DISCARDED

MOVING EARTH

Series Editor: STEVE PARKER

DAVID AND HELEN ORME

QEB Publishing

Designer and Picture Researcher Louise Downey
Project Editor Michael Downey

Copyright © QEB Publishing, Inc. 2010

Published in the United States by
QEB Publishing, Inc.
3 Wrigley, Suite A
Irvine, CA 92618

www.qed-publishing.co.uk

Orme, David, 1948 Mar. 1-
    Moving Earth / David and Helen Orme.
        p. cm. -- (QEB Earth explorer)
    Includes index.
    ISBN 978-1-59566-694-9 (lib. bdg.)
 1. Historical geology--Juvenile literature. 2. Geology--
Juvenile literature. 3. Earth--Juvenile literature. I. Orme,
Helen. II. Title.
    QE29.O763 2011
    551.7--dc22

                            2010005378

Printed in China

Picture Credits

Key: t=top, b=bottom, c=center,
FC=front cover

Corbis 7t Lloyd Cluff/ 22–23 Michael S.
Yamashita/ 23c Bettmann/ 24–25 Anatoly
Maltsev-epa/ 25c Menno Boermans-Aurora
Photos/ 26b Jeremy Horner / 27t STR-epa
Getty Images 10b Paul Chesley / 11b Dario
Mitidieri-Contributor / 13t / 14 Arctic-Images/
14b Travel Pix
NASA 1/ 2–3/ 18br NASA/USGS/Tammy
Becker and Paul Geissler / 30–31/ 32
Photoshot 18–19 VWPics/
Science Photo Library 6–7 Gary Hincks/6t
Gary Hincks/ 9t Mikkel Juul Jensen-Bonnier
Publications/ 8c Christian Darkin/ 16–17 Prof.
Stewart Lowther/ 20t Dr Ken MacDonald/ 20b
Dr Ken MacDonald/ 21 Dr Ken MacDonald/ 22b
Gary Hincks/ 26–27 Gary Hincks/
Shutterstock 4b Shipov Oleg/ 4–5 Jon
Naustdalslid/ 5 Lysithee/ 9c Map Resources/
markrhiggins/ 10–11 Supertrooper/ 12–13
Volodymyr Goinyk/ 12b iNNOCENt/ 13 Caitlin
Mirra/ 15 Gian Corrêa Saléro/ 17b John Hua/
18b gracious_tiger/ 19t Supertrooper/ 24t Juha
Sompinmäki/ 28c Andreas Meyer/ 28 JCElv/ 29
Walter G Arce

Words in bold are
explained in the
Glossary on page 30.

Contents

Moving world

Earth's surface is continually moving. Some changes are sudden, such as a volcanic eruption or an earthquake. Much bigger movements also happen, yet these are so slow we hardly notice.

Changing world

Over millions of years, Earth's surface has changed many times. Rocks have been forced up to form mountains, which have then been worn away by wind and rain. Earthquakes have opened up huge cracks in the Earth's surface and hot volcanic material has covered vast areas of land.

Tell me more!

Nowhere on Earth is the land perfectly still. All land moves at least 0.5 inches (one centimeter) per year, carrying rivers, valleys, hills, and even towns and cities. Many places also move up or down at the same rate.

All parts of a **tectonic plate** move, including the coastline. This area in Sognefjord, Norway, has moved 16 miles (25 kilometers) west in the last 10,000 years.

Cracked surface

All of these changes happen because Earth is not solid rock. Inside, it is partly melted. On the outside, the Earth is like a cracked egg, made of giant curved pieces called tectonic plates. The plates are pushed around by the swirling, partly melted rock beneath. These bump, rub, and crash together.

Venezuela's Angel Falls is the world's highest waterfall, with a height of 3,212 feet (979 meters). It formed when a huge chunk of rock slipped down.

5

Tectonic plates

Earth's outer layer, the crust, is made of jagged-edged tectonic plates. These are constantly on the move, drifting on the part-liquid rock beneath.

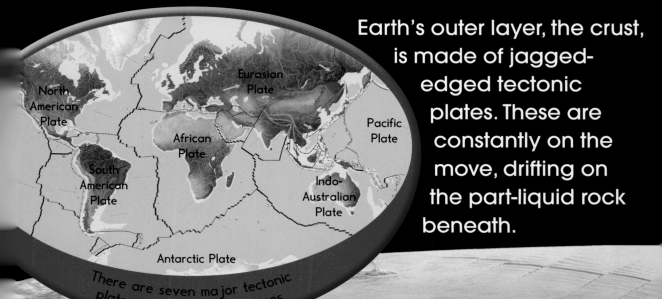

North American Plate

Eurasian Plate

African Plate

South American Plate

Pacific Plate

Indo-Australian Plate

Antarctic Plate

There are seven major tectonic plates and many smaller ones.

Subduction zone, where one plate slides under another

Building mountains

Under Earth's crust is the partly melted **mantle**. This swirls and flows very slowly, carrying the plates along with it. In some places, the plates push against each other and their edges crumple to form mountains and valleys.

Sliding past

At a **transform fault**, two plates slide sideways past each other. This produces cracks in the ground and sometimes earthquakes. At the San Andreas Fault, which lies along the coast of western North America, the Pacific plate slides past the North American plate by more than 0.5 inches (one centimeter) each year.

Tell me more!

The San Andreas Fault is 800 miles (1300 kilometers) long and varies in width from a few feet to hundreds of miles. There have been four big earthquakes along it in the past 150 years.

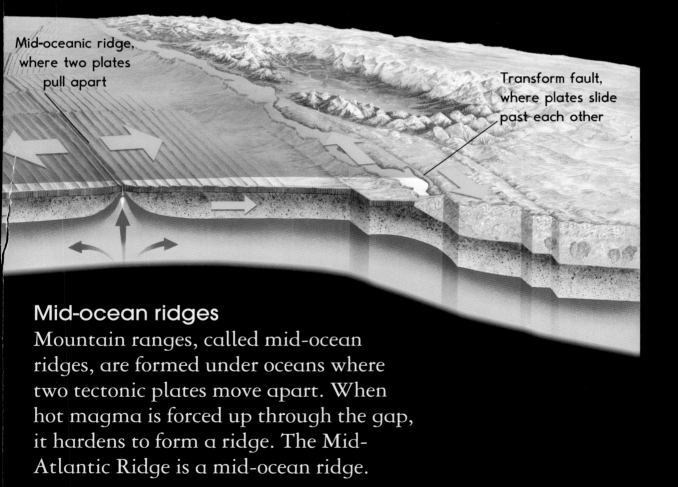

Mid-oceanic ridge, where two plates pull apart

Transform fault, where plates slide past each other

Mid-ocean ridges

Mountain ranges, called mid-ocean ridges, are formed under oceans where two tectonic plates move apart. When hot magma is forced up through the gap, it hardens to form a ridge. The Mid-Atlantic Ridge is a mid-ocean ridge.

Pangaea

Around 200 million years ago, all land on Earth was joined together in one massive **supercontinent** we now call Pangaea.

Pangaea was surrounded by an enormous ocean known as Panthalassa.

One vast land

About 180 million years ago, Pangaea began to split apart. First it broke into two land masses, Laurasia in the north and Gondwana in the south. Then these split into the **continents** we know today. However, these took millions more years to drift to their present positions.

Tell me more!

Pangaea was not the first supercontinent. The Rodinia supercontinent lasted from 1,100 to 750 million years ago. By 600 million years ago, the tectonic plates had changed again to form another supercontinent. This is known as Pannotia.

On the move

How do we know that the supercontinent we call Pangaea really existed? One way is to look at at map of the world to see how the continents may have once fitted together. The east coast of South America fits quite neatly with the west coast of Africa.

Pangaea was breaking up 170 million years ago.

The seven continents in today's positions.

Common fossils

There is also fossil evidence to show that the Pangaean supercontinent once existed. Fossils of the same plants and animals have been found in South America as well as in Africa. This indicates that these two continents were once linked together in one big landmass.

This fish fossil was found in South America and Africa.

9

Ring of Fire

All around the Pacific tectonic plate are earthquake and volcano zones. These make up the "Ring of Fire."

Mapping the plates

Scientists know that where Earth's tectonic plates meet there are likely to be more earthquakes and volcanic eruptions. By keeping a careful record of all the earthquakes and eruptions that occur, they have been able to make a detailed map of the Earth's tectonic plates.

NORTH PACIFIC OC

JAPAN

CHINA

PHILIPPINES

INDONESIA

AUSTRALIA

Tell me more!

As earthquakes are common in Japan, each month the country's schoolchildren take part in an earthquake drill. Those on lower floors of the school get under their desks and hold on tightly to the desk's legs. Children on upper floors practice using a chute to escape the building quickly.

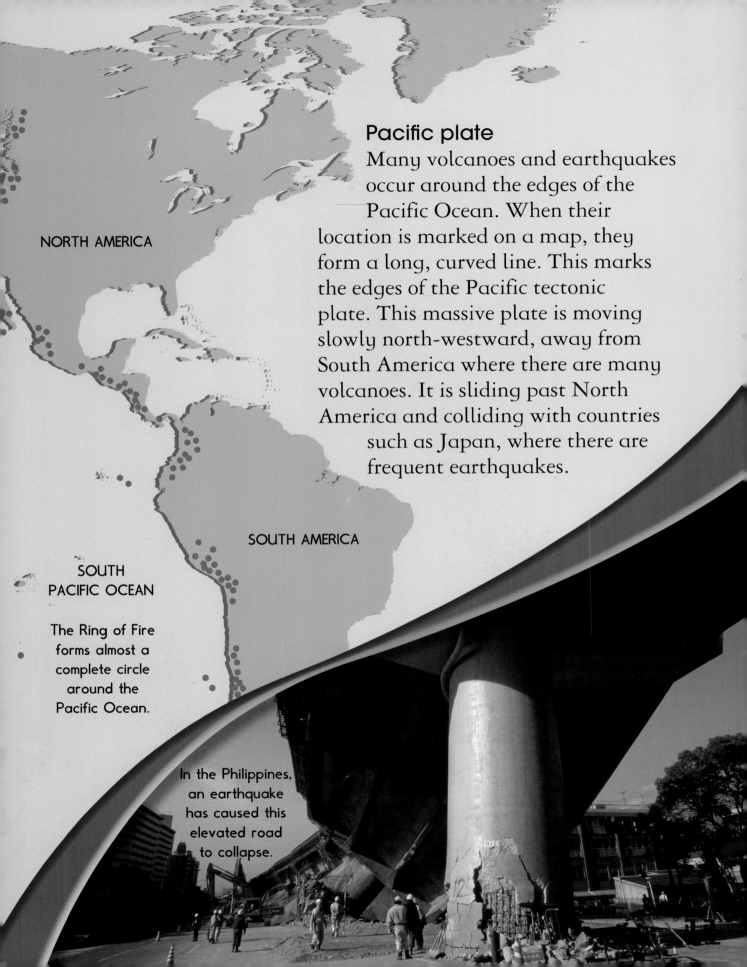

NORTH AMERICA

SOUTH AMERICA

SOUTH
PACIFIC OCEAN

The Ring of Fire
forms almost a
complete circle
around the
Pacific Ocean.

Pacific plate

Many volcanoes and earthquakes occur around the edges of the Pacific Ocean. When their location is marked on a map, they form a long, curved line. This marks the edges of the Pacific tectonic plate. This massive plate is moving slowly north-westward, away from South America where there are many volcanoes. It is sliding past North America and colliding with countries such as Japan, where there are frequent earthquakes.

In the Philippines, an earthquake has caused this elevated road to collapse.

Mountains

Mountains can be formed by volcanic activity as well as from movements in the tectonic plates.

Fold mountains

A type of mountain called a fold mountain is formed when tectonic plates squeeze against each other. When this happens, rock layers in Earth's crust are pushed up, which causes them to fold and then crack. New fold mountains usually have sharp, jagged peaks.

The Himalayas began to form about 70 million years ago.

Volcanic plugs

Mountains are also formed from the remains of volcanoes. These mountains, which are called **volcanic plugs**, are made when magma fills up a volcano's vent and hardens into rock. After millions of years, the outer part of the volcano may be worn away, leaving the plug behind.

Edinburgh Castle in Scotland, U.K., was built on a volcanic plug.

Tell me more!

The highest place on Earth is the top of Mount Everest, which is 29,029 feet (8848 meters) above sea level. The world's tallest mountain, however, is Mauna Kea in Hawaii, an extinct or dead volcano. Much of it is under water. Its total height from seabed to summit is about 29,850 feet (9100 meters).

Dome mountains

Sometimes, huge blocks of rock in Earth's crust are pushed up by the hot **magma** below. If the magma cannot find a way out through the crust, it may push up a weak part of the crust to form what is known as a dome mountain. This type of mountain, such as Half Dome mountain in California, often has a flattened top.

California's Half Dome mountain was formed flat on one side.

13

What is a volcano?

Volcanoes form when red-hot runny rock, called magma, pushes up from far below and out through Earth's crust.

Volcanic mountain

A volcano is a place in Earth's crust where material from deep inside Earth forces its way out. Because this molten material is under immense pressure, it can also form a mountain. This happens when rock layers are pushed up by trapped magma, creating what is known as a volcanic mountain. When the volcano erupts, **lava** and ash from the volcano can add to the size of the volcanic mountain.

Lava from an erupting volcano flows down its slopes like a red-hot river of rock.

Tell me more!

Many people live close to active volcanoes. It sounds a dangerous thing to do, but the soil around the volcano is often rich in **minerals** and good for growing **crops**.

Inside a volcano

When lava, ash, and other materials shoot out of a volcano's crater, the volcano is said to be erupting. Before an eruption, hot magma rises through Earth's mantle and collects in a large pool—the magma chamber. When the pressure here is great enough, magma is forced up a pipe called the conduit. It then bursts out as liquid rock called lava.

Gas and
ash cloud

Vent

Lava

Crater

Conduit
(pipe)

Magma
chamber

Living with volcanoes

When there is a massive and unexpected volcanic eruption, the lives and safety of thousands of people may be at risk.

Extreme danger

The biggest danger for people from a volcanic eruption is not from falling rocks. Nor it is from the rivers of red-hot lava that travel downhill at speeds of up to 62 miles (100 kilometers) per hour. The greatest danger comes from poisonous clouds known as pyroclastic flows. These clouds can travel downhill at 430 miles per hour (700 kilometers per hour) and may reach temperatures of 1,800 degrees Fahrenheit (1,000 degrees Celsius)!

In 1980, the eruption of Mount St. Helens in Washington State killed 57 people.

Tell me more!

One of the biggest eruptions in history was Mount Krakatau in Indonesia. In 1883, the whole volcanic island blew apart. More than 35,000 people died in the explosion and from the giant waves, or **tsunamis**, that it caused.

Seeking safety

Today, scientists can sometimes warn people living near an active volcano that it is about to erupt, so that they can quickly move to safe areas. The signs they look for include small earthquakes, the ground around a volcano becoming hot, and **tremors** in the ground.

Deadly clouds

Anyone unlucky enough to be caught up in a pyroclastic flow would probably be killed instantly. This happened in the town of Pompeii in Italy. In AD 79, Mount Vesuvius erupted and covered the entire town and its doomed inhabitants in deadly volcanic ash. The town, which was completely covered, lay hidden for almost 1,600 years.

A plaster cast of a victim of the tragedy in Pompeii.

Super-volcanoes

Super-volcanoes are giant volcanoes covering vast areas. If one were to erupt, it could endanger all life on Earth.

Massive destruction

A super-volcano forms where magma tries to force its way up through the crust but cannot break through. If this were to happen, more and more pressure would build up over a wider and wider area. At some point, perhaps, half a continent may explode! The last super-volcano eruption took place many thousands of years ago.

Warning signs

When large pools of magma collect deep down, hot springs and **geysers** may appear on Earth's surface. These features could show that a super-volcano is building up beneath.

White Dome Geyser, in Yellowstone National Park gushes out a hot spray up to 30 feet (9 meters) high.

Tell me more!

Earth is not the only planet to have super-volcanoes. They have been spotted on some of the moons of Jupiter and Saturn.

A super-volcano on Io, a moon of Jupiter.

Scientists do not know when the next devastating super-volcanic eruption will take place.

The Siberian Traps, Russia

Yellowstone, Wyoming

Long Valley Caldera, California

Valles Calderas, New Mexico

Kyushu, Southern Japan

Aira Caldera, Kagoshima

Taupo Volcano, New Zealand

Scientists believe that there are seven sites around the world that could become super-volcanoes in the future.

World event

If a super-volcano were to erupt, huge areas of Earth would be covered with lava and ash. The effects would be felt all around the world and could last for many years. The Lake Toba super-volcano in Sumatra, Indonesia, exploded 75,000 years ago. Temperatures around the world dropped, and more than half the people in the world died.

Undersea volcanoes

As well as the volcanoes on land, there are many more deep under the sea.

Rock shapes

Undersea volcanoes are similar to those on land. They occur along the edges of tectonic plates and they erupt lava, ash, and gases. Lava cools very quickly in sea water, forming strange rock shapes on the seabed.

Undersea lava hardens as bulges called pillow lava.

Strange crabs, fish, and worms live around deep-sea hydrothermal vents

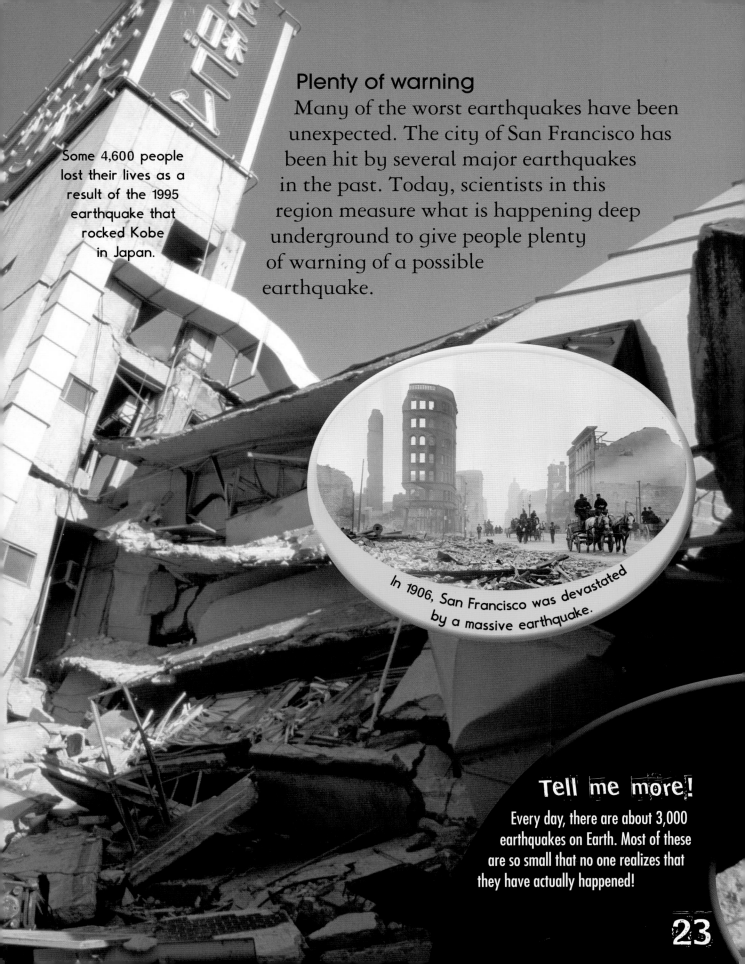

Some 4,600 people lost their lives as a result of the 1995 earthquake that rocked Kobe in Japan.

Plenty of warning

Many of the worst earthquakes have been unexpected. The city of San Francisco has been hit by several major earthquakes in the past. Today, scientists in this region measure what is happening deep underground to give people plenty of warning of a possible earthquake.

In 1906, San Francisco was devastated by a massive earthquake.

Tell me more!

Every day, there are about 3,000 earthquakes on Earth. Most of these are so small that no one realizes that they have actually happened!

Landslides

The landscape can change when parts of mountains or cliffs fall to the land or the sea below. These are known as landslides or landslips.

Whole hillsides can slide away.

Causes of landslides

Landslides can be caused by earthquakes, by underground water during wet weather, or by the wearing away of land to leave overhanging rocks. Landslides also happen when too many trees on hills and mountains are cut down. This can cause an entire side of a hill or mountain to slip down.

Deadly mudslides

When soil is very wet, it turns into mud. This is when a mudslide can strike. Mudslides, which can also carry tons of rocks, may reach speeds of 50 miles (80 kilometers) per hour. Because mudslides are unpredictable, they can be extremely dangerous.

Danger to life

An avalanche is a mass of snow that rushes down a mountainside. It can destroy buildings that lie in its path. Avalanches often start after heavy winter snow. They can be triggered by a simple human activity, such as snowboarding, or by natural events, such as high winds. In mountain regions, avalanches pose the greatest danger to human life.

In 2002, a huge 20-mile (30-kilometer) landslide in the Koban Valley, Russia, killed 125 people.

Avalanches travel faster than people can run, or even ski.

Tell me more!

Landslides into the sea can cause tsunamis. Some scientists think that a volcanic eruption could start a massive landslide in the Canary Islands, which may then create a huge tsunami. This giant wave could rush across the Atlantic Ocean and devastate the east coast of America.

Tsunamis

A tsunami is a giant wave that rushes up from the sea and onto the land. The massive wall of water can destroy anything that lies in its path.

What causes tsunamis?

A tsunami may be triggered by a violent earthquake that pushes up the seabed. It could also be caused by an underwater volcano or even by a huge landslide into the sea.

Undersea earthquake

Low, fast surface wave

Even a small tsunami can wash away cars and break up roads.

Wall of water

A tsunami usually starts deep in the ocean. At first, it looks like an ordinary wave on the ocean's surface. People on ships far out at sea do not even notice that something is happening. At this point, the tsunami is moving very fast. As the sea becomes shallower around the coast, the tsunami slows down and becomes much higher.

The 2004 Indian Ocean tsunami killed more than 220,000 people.

Hitting the shore

Tsunamis can rise to the height of a two-story building just before they hit the shore. When a tsunami finally breaks, the force of the water is so strong it destroys buildings and can move heavy objects far inland.

Wave builds higher

Wave slows down

Wave breaks onto shore

A tsunami may travel many hundreds of miles at sea before it crashes onto the shore.

Tell me more!

Can animals tell that a tsunami is going to happen before we can? Just before the 2004 Indian Ocean tsunami, people saw animals behaving oddly. Elephants rushed to higher ground and dogs refused to go on the beach.

When Earth shakes

The biggest movements on Earth happen when giant rocks from space, such as **asteroids**, **meteorites**, and **comets**, smash into the planet.

Sudden impact

About every 10 million years, on average, a massive chunk of rock more than 3 miles (5 kilometers) across hurtles from space into Earth. What happens depends on how fast it travels, the angle at which it strikes, and where it hits—in the mountains, on a tectonic plate edge, or in the sea.

Tell me more!

A meteorite impact 65 million years ago may have wiped out the dinosaurs. Scientists have discovered the remains of an 590-foot (180-meter) wide crater on the coast of Mexico. This crater, called Chicxulub, may mark the site where the meteorite struck.

Earth on the move

A big impact sets off many natural disasters. Stuck tectonic plates slip, triggering massive earthquakes. The cracked crust allows more volcanoes to erupt, and even super-volcanoes. Huge tsunamis crash onto shores around the world. The whole Earth seems on the move.

Almost 65 million years ago, dinosaurs and **pterosaurs** fled the giant meteorite that wiped them out and ravaged Earth.

Future strike

Great impacts are becoming rarer as many of the big space rocks in the Solar System have already crashed into other planets or their moons. From what we know, Earth's next big collision could be in 800 years—and even that is unlikely.

At 4,000 feet (1,200 meters) across, Barringer Crater in Arizona was formed by a 160-foot (50-meter) meteorite 40,000 years ago.

Glossary

Asteroid Huge lump of space rock many miles across, moving around the Sun.

Comet Big ball of ice and dust, moving around the Sun.

Continent Very large area, or mass, of land.

Crops Plants grown by people for food or products.

Epicenter Place on the surface above the center of an earthquake, where it is felt most strongly.

Geyser A spring that erupts hot water and steam, caused by a magma pool close to the surface.

Lava When magma erupts from a volcano, it is known as lava.

Magma Hot, semi-liquid rock that makes up Earth's outer core.

Mantle A layer between the Earth's crust and its core.

Meteorite Large lump of rock traveling through space.

Mineral Natural substance that makes up rocks.

Pterosaurs Flying creatures that thrived during the Age of Dinosaurs but are now all extinct.

Subduction zone Area where one tectonic plate is pushed down under the edge of another.

Supercontinent Vast area of land made of two or more continents connected together.

Tectonic plate Large curved section of the Earth's outer layer, the crust.

Tsunami Massive, powerful wave set off by an earthquake, volcano, or landslide.

Transform fault Area where one tectonic plate slides past another.

Tremor Shaking or vibrations.

Volcanic plug Central part of a volcano, where the lava has gone very hard.

Index

Ideas for parents and teachers

Here are some fun and practical activities children can do at home or school.

Supercontinent puzzle
Using a map of the world, or perhaps a photocopy of a map, cut out the Earth's major land masses. Try to fit these land masses together to create the supercontinent Pangaea, which existed on Earth 200 million years ago.

Create a mountain
For this activity you will need modelling clay, in different colors
• Build up the modelling clay in flat layers using the different colors. These colors represent the different layers, or strata, of Earth's crust.
• Gently push the layers from each end, recreating the effect of fold mountains building as two tectonic plates collide.

Simulate an earthquake
You will need some stiff card stock, a flat tray, and some play sand.
• Place two pieces of card stock side by side on the tray.
• Cover the cardboard with slightly damp sand. Pat the sand down firmly.
• Slide the cards against each other, or pull them apart, to simulate the effects of an earthquake on Earth's surface. The two pieces of card stock represent adjacent tectonic plates.

Mapping events
Collect news reports from newspapers and the Internet on world events, such as earthquakes, volcanic eruptions, and tsunamis. Plot these events on a map of the world, or create a disaster timeline.

Volcano diary
Find out more about the eruption of Mount Vesuvius in 79 BC that destroyed the ancient Roman towns of Pompeii and Herculaneum. Write an account of the eruption as if you were a survivor who witnessed the tragedy as it happened.

Information poster
Design a poster informing people what they should do in the event of an earthquake or a tsunami alert.

Volcano glossary
Create a large, labeled color illustration of an erupting volcano. This should be large enough to hang on a wall. Use the illustration on page 15 of this book as a starting point. Consider showing added details in your cross-section illustration, such as the the layers of lava and ash that build up after each eruption.